30s & 40s

IN

JOHN GUY

COUNTRY LIFE

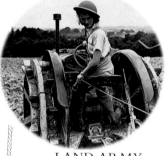

LAND ARMY

This view of a typical farming scene in the 1940s shows a woman working on a farm as part of the Government's 'Women's Land Army' campaign. In the early years of the war Britain faced both a food and labour shortage. Many farm labourers had joined the armed forces and women were encouraged to take their jobs.

The two decades of the 1930s and 1940s were dominated by two major events that affected everyone's lives, rich or poor: namely the Depression (1929 to the mid 1930s) and the Second World War (1939 to 1945). Together they created one of the bleakest eras in British history. Life in country areas was significantly affected by the Depression, more subtly perhaps than the great industrial towns of the North, but changes were brought about during this period that still affect rural lives today. The first change was the sudden fall in grain prices on the world market, which made it uneconomic for many farmers to grow food. The second, and perhaps greatest change, came during the Second World War. The German U-boat campaign to disrupt merchant ships crossing the Atlantic caused major food shortages in Britain. Farmers were forced to employ more intensive growing methods to cope with demand, which resulted, in the years after the war, in farms with considerably reduced workforces. Jobs on the land became scarcer after the war.

OLD WAYS

Prior to the Second World War, many of the traditional tasks on the farm were still performed by horse-power, such as ploughing. Today, heavy horses are usually only seen at special agricultural displays and have long since ceased to be a familiar part of the countryside.

A FORGOTTEN INDUSTRY

Oast houses were once a familiar scene in the South-east. They were drying kilns for hops, grown for the brewing industry to make beer. Traditionally many Londoners from the East End spent their annual 'holiday' in Kent gathering in the hops, living in makeshift camps on the farms. Sadly, mechanization and cheaper imports have meant the decline of the hop industry. Most of the oast houses have now been converted into private residences.

'DIG FOR VICTORY'

During the war the Government introduced many special campaigns, complete with catchy slogans, to encourage people to pull together to defeat the enemy. One of the most successful of these was the 'Dig for Victory' campaign, when anyone who had a garden was encouraged to grow their own food. Allotments, introduced during the First World War, became common once again and country dwellers who generally had larger gardens, were encouraged to grow as much food as possible to help overcome local food shortages.

THE KING INTERVENES

The mining valleys of South Wales were badly affected during the Depression as there was often no alternative work. In 1936, shortly before he abdicated, Edward VIII visited the valleys, and protested to the Government that '...*something must be done to find these people work.*'

COUNTRY SPORTS

Traditional country pursuits, such as shooting and fishing, enjoyed increased popularity in the 1930s and 40s, especially during the war years when meat was in short supply and rationed. The wealthy engaged in organized shoots while the poor may have caught the odd wild rabbit to supplement the meagre family diet.

LIFE IN TOWNS

CHEAP HOUSING

Most of the housing for the working classes was built in town centres, close to the factories and other places of industry. Some local authorities built a stock of houses, which they rented out to the less well-off, but most working-class houses were built by speculative landlords, who rented the properties out for low weekly rents.

*A*lthough Britain was still suffering from the effects of the Depression throughout the 1930s, from about 1937 there were signs of improvement. As the heavier, more traditional industries of the North went into decline, so the newer, lighter industries, such as the manufacturing of electrical appliances, gradually began to grow. The more affluent South-east felt less of the effect of the Depression and recovered quickest. By 1933 the National Grid had been completed, bringing electricity to those who could afford it, and most towns had tarmacked roads throughout, to accommodate the increased use of motor cars. Most towns also had their own gas works, providing a source of light and heat to many homes.

LOOKOUT IN THE BLACKOUT

BLACKOUTS

During the war it became every citizen's duty to black out all windows at night with heavy curtains and blinds, so as not to present any target to passing German bombers. Street lamps and even vehicle head-lamps were forbidden and special wardens patrolled the streets to make sure everyone complied.

SUBURBIA

The growing middle classes opted to live in the new suburbs that began to appear on the outskirts of the towns, and commute into the towns to work. Mostly employed in regular, professional occupations, they could usually secure a mortgage and buy their own houses, often for less than the working classes paid in rent. Semi-detached houses with gardens became popular at this time, as distinct from the terraced rows of working-class homes, with their back yards. A typical, three-bedroomed house in the 1930s cost between £400–£500 and could be secured with a £5 deposit and weekly payments of just 60p–70p.

INDUSTRIAL POLLUTION

The Depression of the 1930s brought obvious hardship to those who lived and worked in the heavily industrialized towns. Sheffield, shown here, was once the centre of the British steel industry but as such industries declined, many of the dirty and out-dated factories were demolished, making way for newer, cleaner industries. The changes were slow but, now, the appalling pollution caused by such industrial plants is largely a thing of the past.

HEALTH IMPROVEMENTS

Sanitation in towns improved dramatically in the 1930s. By that time, all towns had a mains water supply and improved drainage systems which drastically reduced the incidences of water-borne diseases. Improved health care, such as iron-lungs for polio sufferers, and x-ray equipment, became common features of municipal hospitals.

NEW TOWN PLANS

Hitler's bombing campaigns of the Second World War had an unexpected effect on the townscapes of Britain in the years that followed. The first task was to clear up the mess, but then began the rebuilding of demolished towns. Many town centres owe their present open-plans to this post-war rebuilding.

MORRIS MINOR 1000

Now better than ever   IMPROVED PERFORMANCE · INCREASED SAFETY

HAPPY MOTORING

During the 1930s motoring became very popula[r] with the upper and middle classes. A typical sma[ll] family saloon car in 1935, such as the Austin 10 [or] Morris Minor – a later model shown here – cost around £120. These were the two dominant car[s] marketed in Britain at the time.

A PLACE IN THE SUN

Holidays abroad were popular with the rich, as a means of escape from the gloom of the 1930s. The British-built *Queen Mary* had her maiden voyage in 1936. At that time she was the largest ocean-going liner in service and regularly plied the North Atlantic to New York.

THE STORY R.M.S. QUEEN M[ARY]

QUEEN·MARY

A DESCRIPTIVE SOUVENIR, LAV[...] OF THE WORLD'S GR[...]

'BRITAIN CAN MAKE IT'

Immediately following the end of the Second World War, British manufacturers launched a 'Britain Can Make It' exhibition, to show off the expertise of our new manufacturing industries.
Many new designs and inventions were presented, such as this bicycle boasting a dynamo and motor, suspension, shaft drive, electric bell and miniature radio. It was typical of the new ideas being developed at the time as Britain's factories switched from making armaments to luxury items, to feed the growing consumer market.

ROYAL FAVOURITES

George VI and his wife, Elizabeth Bowes-Lyon, were amongst our most popular monarchs. They endeared themselves to the British public when they refused to leave England during the Second World War, even after Buckingham Palace itself was bombed in 1940. The royal family spent the duration of the war principally in the Royal Lodge, a modest residence in the grounds of Windsor Castle. Princess Elizabeth (the present queen) is shown second from the left.

LIFE FOR THE RICH

By the 1930s, few middle-class families could afford to employ servants and even the wealthiest families had considerably reduced their staffs. This trend continued during the war years and never returned to the days when a virtual army of servants was employed as in the rich households of Victorian and Edwardian times. There were by now many new, labour-saving devices that, in theory, removed the necessity for servants. Most of the well-off never experienced the full hardship of the Depression. Even during the war years, those with money could still manage to buy the goods they needed on the 'black market'. However, many of the largest houses of the rich were requisitioned at this time by the armed services.

LIFE GOES ON

The rich enjoyed a relatively unchanged lifestyle throughout the troubled period of the 1930s and 40s. Most were white-collar workers and were mostly unaffected by the worst ravages of the Depression. Many still enjoyed a busy social calendar with plenty of time for dances and functions.

THE HIGH LIFE

The 1930s saw many innovations in the field of interior house designs, with the introduction of new materials such as chrome and bakelite. This view of a lounge in a typical middle-class house is not too dissimilar from modern interiors. Many wealthy people decorated their homes in the new, modern artistic styles, such as Art Deco.

THE POOR AT HOME

SIMPLE PLEASURES

Despite the obvious hardships of the period, there existed a kind of camaraderie that had seldom been witnessed before. Beer was cheap (about 2p a pint) and many men met in the local pub for a chat or to play games, such as darts or dominoes. Pubs were mostly the preserve of men, although women would sometimes accompany their husbands.

The poor were affected most by the Great Depression of the 1930s. Most were unskilled labourers who could not easily find alternative work when factories closed down. The Depression began on 24 October 1929 when the New York Stock Exchange collapsed. The price of wheat in America suddenly fell, followed by most other commodities, causing many businessmen and governments throughout the developed world to lose fortunes. Unemployment rose rapidly throughout the next 10 years as Britain's (and the world's) staple industries collapsed. In 1936, unemployed ship builders from Jarrow, in north-east England, where nearly 80 percent of the workers were unemployed, marched to London to protest to the Government.

MASS PRODUCTION

This view shows men working on a production line in a car assembly factory in Oxford, around 1930. Many of the traditional industries, like ship building, coal mining and steel works, were in severe decline after the Great Depression. Many men had to resort to monotonous, unskilled work in factories, such as this, earning an average wage in the late 1930s of about £400 per year.

CHEAP DAY RETURN

Most poor people could not afford to take holidays. To make ends meet, most men worked a six-day week and few jobs paid holiday money. When money allowed, working-class families might go to the local beach on a day trip. They usually travelled by train, and few ventured very far from home.

BARMOUTH NORTH WALES
FOR MOUNTAIN, SAND & SEA
Illustrated Guide 6d, Heulwen Tourist Office, Barmouth
TRAVEL BY TRAIN

THE GREAT DEPRESSION

The effects of the Great Depression were felt for the next 10 years and only really came to an end at the outbreak of the Second World War. The principle hardship was mass unemployment. By the mid-1930s unemployment reached 3 million in Britain, the highest recorded total ever. Those who were unemployed did receive some (albeit minimal) financial help from the Government, about £1.50 a week per family. Jobs were often given out on a daily basis and workers had to queue at factory gates each morning in search of work.

POOR PAY

Another major effect of the Great Depression was the reduction in wages, caused by falling output and demand for commodities. Working conditions also deteriorated, prompting some workers to go on strike for better pay and conditions. Strikers received no pay and only minimal compensation from the unions and so most workers would only strike as a last resort. Because so many people were looking for jobs, some unscrupulous employers deliberately kept wages low and threatened to sack strikers, offering their jobs to the unemployed.

BASIC ACCOMMODATION

Most working-class homes during the 1930s and 40s were rented, usually from private landlords. There was little spare money for luxuries, as most of the wages were spent on food and rent. Many poorer families still cooked on open ranges. The lucky ones had small gas cookers, like this one, which were more efficient.

DRIED FOOD

Another method of food preservation that gained popularity at this time was dehydration. The liquid content of foods such as mashed potato and eggs (shown here) is withdrawn and the remaining food powdered. It is reconstituted by simply adding hot water. Powdered egg was a main ingredient during the war years.

COFFEE BLENDS

Coffee first appeared in England in the 17th century but, for a long time, it was considered an expensive luxury. In Britain coffee has always been less favoured than tea, but by the 1930s companies, such as Lyons, offered a range of blends by grinding and mixing various types of bean, principally from Africa and South America. During the war, when coffee was in short supply, various alternatives were introduced, such as roasted chicory roots. Instant coffee was first marketed in America in 1937.

THE COMMON MAN'S DRINK

It was around 1930 that tea ceased to be a luxury, confined to the upper classes, and became more easily available to all. Tea production had increased enormously in the Empire. Tea, principally from India and China, soon became the staple beverage of the working classes.

INCREASED YIELDS

Until the late 1930s the only form of crop fertilizer was manure and other organic substances. During the food shortage crisis of the war, however, scientists developed chemical fertilizers that increased crop yields by artificial means. The first such fertilizers were used in 1940 and by 1944 their use was widespread.

FOOD & DRINK

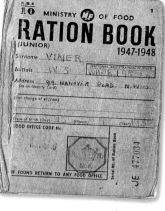

Throughout history, desperate times usually give way to human ingenuity. Such was the case during the Second World War, when the German U-boat campaign against the allied merchant fleets caused massive food shortages. The British and American Governments set to work to research food technology, food preservation and chemical additives to supplement the meagre diet. An underfed nation would not be able to resist the German onslaught and so no expense was spared. This invaluable work formed the backbone of today's high-technology food industry, with its emphasis on preservation, genetic engineering and microbiology.

RATIONING

Rationing was not new to the British people, it had first been introduced during the First World War. It was introduced again in 1940 to both conserve provisions and to ensure a fair division. Coupons were issued, which had to be presented when purchasing items such as food, clothing and petrol. Queues became a feature of rationing, people trying to ensure they got their fair share before the supplies ran out. Rationing continued after the war; clothes became unrationed in 1949 but food remained on ration until 1954. If you were invited to dine at someone else's house, it was usual to take your rations with you, rather than use your host's food.

PROCESSED FOODS

Scientists involved in food technology during the war greatly improved the methods used for drying and canning food. Processed food could be stored safely for long periods, often with the addition of chemicals to prevent mould growth and deterioration.

PASTIMES

During the Depression, few could afford to spend much time or money on leisure activities. However, the years that followed, although difficult and at times gloomy, somehow brought out the best in human spirit. No-one knew when their life might suddenly end so many opted for a 'live-for-the-moment' attitude and enjoyed life with zeal. Much of the entertainment was homespun, but people enjoyed going to the cinema, the pub and the local dance-hall or listening to the radio. After the war a new sense of hope swept the nation. British seaside resorts, many of which had been closed to the public during the war, enjoyed a veritable boom as people began to travel more.

RADIO

By the 1930s radio was one of the most popular forms of home entertainment. In Britain, broadcasts were transmitted by the BBC to provide a range of programmes including music, news bulletins, comedy and talk shows. Families regularly sat around the radio listening to serial stories. Edward VIII announced his abdication over the radio in 1936 and on 3 September 1939 the British Prime Minister, Neville Chamberlain, announced that Britain was at war with Germany.

THEATRE GOING

Much of the entertainment in the 1930s and 40s was live. People enjoyed going to the theatre and every town in Britain could usually boast at least one, but often several theatres, showing anything from comedy reviews to serious drama. Music Hall was also very popular. With the growing popularity of films, many theatres closed down after the 1940s or were converted into cinemas.

A DAY AT THE RACES

Horse-racing and dog-racing were very popular in the 1930s and 40s, the former mostly frequented by the middle and upper classes, the latter by the working classes. During the Second World War many sports went into decline, partly because many of the players were called up to armed service and partly because many of the sports grounds were put to other uses. The Oval cricket ground, for example, was used as a prisoner-of-war camp.

A NIGHT AT THE FLICKS

During the 1930s and 40s, theatre and cinema provided an escape from grim reality. Sometimes shows and films had to be staged during the day because of black-out restrictions. Cinemas regularly pulled in audiences of 25–30 million each week. Favourite films were Hollywood movies, such as *The Wizard of Oz*, which starred Judy Garland and was the first film produced in Technicolor. The British film industry was also active at this time, mainly producing morale-boosting wartime dramas. Cinemas also showed up-to-date newsreel films which gave people an idea of how the war was progressing.

FIRST TELEVISION SERVICE

Television was a new and exciting entertainment medium in the 1930s, although only the very rich could afford one and broadcasts were limited. During the war, transmissions stopped altogether. Equipment used to transmit the signal (and even the television sets themselves) was huge by today's standards. This view shows the first television station at Alexandra Palace. The world's first television service was broadcast in 1936 by the BBC.

THE LIGHT FANTASTIC

A popular pastime for people of all classes was dancing. Ballroom dancing was very popular, but at about this time the forerunner of modern dancing began to appear. Young couples danced to the beat of popular melodies, the music provided by swing and jazz bands. Many of the musicians were serving military bandsmen who entertained the armed services abroad or civilians when at home on leave. One of the most popular dance crazes of the early 1940s was the Jitterbug, imported from America.

FASHION

Clothing became much brighter and more varied as the 1930s progressed, until the advent of the Second World War. Many of the more formal looks of the 1920s were superseded by more elegant clothes. New types of fasteners, like zips and press-studs, made it easier to get into and out of clothes, which greatly affected their design. During this time no one style held sway, but women in particular felt free to wear any style they chose.

There was a greater use of colour, even for men, who now wore pastel-coloured shirts instead of the more usual white. Hollywood was a great influence on fashion at this time with both men and women trying to copy the great movie stars.

HAIRSTYLES

By the 1930s, short bobs were often replaced with long, wavy hair, often permed into curls. For men, hair dressings in the form of oils and creams to create a smooth, swept-back look became fashionable.

SHEER ELEGANCE

Before the invention of nylon in 1935, stockings were usually made of expensive materials such as silk. Nylon, an artificial material, became very popular, but went into short supply during the war years. Stockings at that time had a seam running up the back of the leg and it became fashionable for women to paint a black line up the back of their legs to imitate nylon stockings.

PLAIN & PATRIOTIC

During the Second World War it was considered unpatriotic to waste money and precious resources on fashion. Even turn-ups on trousers were replaced with plain legs. Most clothing had to be purchased using clothing coupons during the war. Shortages of cloth and rationing meant that clothing had to be practical and multi-purpose. Following the end of the war, most people welcomed the return to more colourful and fashionable clothes, when most of the earlier styles of the 1930s were revived.

MAKING DO

During the war, people were encouraged to make do with the clothing they had and mend it rather than replace it. People were encouraged to make their own clothes from recycled materials, using pattern books, as shown here. Frivolity and flamboyance were frowned upon and most clothing was of a plain, utility nature.

FOOTLOOSE

The early 1930s saw some quite extraordinary new designs in footwear, especially for ladies, such as platform soles and wedge heels. During the war years footwear became more functional, designed for comfort and practicality rather than for elegance. The Government encouraged people to repair their old shoes rather than waste valuable resources on buying new ones.

ART & ARCHITECTURE

PICASSO (1881–1973)

Pablo Picasso has often been described as representing the spirit of the age and influenced many modern artists. He was certainly one of the most prolific and versatile artists in Europe at this time. Born in Spain he did much of his work in France. In addition to being a painter of some renown, he was also a sculptor, designer and graphic artist.

*D*uring the war there was a huge upturn of interest in the arts. The Government set up the Council for the Encouragement of Music and the Arts (CEMA) which, after the war, became known as the Arts Council. Theatre, ballet and classical music tours around the country were sponsored to take art to the people. Especially popular were concerts organized for the troops and war workers. Some of the larger towns outside London (such as Bournemouth and Birmingham) began their own symphony orchestras, which still thrive today. The most popular style in art and design was Art Deco, which has greatly influenced many modern styles with its bold, functional yet imaginative styles.

BENJAMIN BRITTEN (1913–76)

One of the most popular British composers of the time was Benjamin Britten, who revived interest in opera with his *Peter Grimes* and other pieces. He also composed a number of works for children, including *The Young Person's Guide to the Orchestra*.

RECEPTION OFFICE

ARCHITECTURE

Before the war, architecture was dominated by two main styles, Art Deco and Modernist. The former was usually reserved for large buildings, such as the spectacular Hoover building (left). The latter frequently used concrete, steel and glass. Buildings in this style were often more functional. After the war, the emphasis was on planning whole new housing estates and town centres as a single, overall plan. The use of steel girders and reinforced or pre-stressed concrete (in which the floors carry the strength of a building and not the walls) saw the construction of the first high-rise buildings.

SOMERSET MAUGHAM

William Somerset Maugham (1874-1965) was a great English novelist, playwright and short-story writer, who was particularly prolific at this time. His style of writing has been described as 'realist' and included such works as *Of Human Bondage* and *The Moon and Sixpence*.

HENRY MOORE (1898-1986)

Henry Moore was commissioned to paint a series of pictures to illustrate the effect of the Second World War on Britain. He often chose the more mundane and unusual as the inspiration for his paintings, such as the cramped living conditions in the underground stations of London, used as bomb shelters. He is more famous today for his unique style of sculpture. This statue called *Composition* was produced by him for the 'Art for the People Exhibition'.

HEALTH & MEDICINE

X-RAYS

The discovery of x-rays was made by Wilhelm Röntgen in 1895. Initially it was used to take 'photographs' of the inside of the body to enable doctors to make a diagnosis without the need for surgery, but by the 1930s, x-rays were also used in the treatment of certain diseases, such as cancer, certain skin complaints and even ringworm.

*I*n 1948 the National Health Service, the first fully state-funded health service in the world, was introduced. Prior to that, the level of treatment received by patients varied enormously from region to region and was often dependent on one's ability to pay. By paying for a national level of health care from taxes, the British Government was able to guarantee the same level of treatment for all. Also, by controlling the funds centrally, including the training of doctors and nurses, the general standards of health care and medical research increased dramatically.

PARENTS
should know about this—

METROPOLITAN LIFE INSURANCE COMPANY

PREVENTATIVE MEASURES

In the 1930s an education programme was launched to convince parents to have their children immunized against common, yet serious, childhood ailments such as diphtheria, a chronic throat infection that was a major cause of death amongst children in this period.

HOSPITAL CARE

Before the introduction of the National Health Service, hospitals in Britain were owned and managed in one of three main ways: by local authorities; by a charity or other non-profit making association; or privately run by a doctor, or group of doctors, for profit. The level of care varied enormously, not only between these three categories, but also according to where you lived. Poor, working-class areas often provided only basic treatment, while the best care was available to those who could afford private treatment.

TUBERCULOSIS

Until the 1940s the only
effective treatment for
tuberculosis, a debilitating
and often fatal disease, was rest
and fresh air, often in sanatoriums
located in remote country areas.
In 1944 the powerful antibiotic,
streptomycin, was developed, followed by several others, which
brought about an effective cure. For example in 1946, 900 girls
aged between 15-19 died of TB; by 1961 the number was just nine.

THE FIRST ANTIBIOTICS

Penicillin was first discovered by Sir Alexander
Fleming in 1928, although it could not be used in
medicine until it had been successfully isolated
and tested. It was first used on patients to
destroy bacteria in 1941 and was the
forerunner of many of today's antibiotic
drugs used in the fight against disease.

KEEPING GERMS
AT BAY

Joseph Lister established the use
of antiseptic methods during
surgery in 1867, and such methods
soon became adopted in many other
medical procedures. The problem was that
the application of antiseptics to infected parts of the
body also damaged healthy tissue surrounding the infection.
In the 1930s aseptic methods of treatment were more fully
developed, which eliminated bacterial infection during
surgery by creating a sterile environment in which to
perform operations.

LOVE & MARRIAGE

The Depression, followed almost immediately by the Second World War, must have filled many people with a sense of foreboding, some adopting a 'live for the moment' attitude with little regard for the consequences. This continued after the war with many feeling that they no longer had to accept things as they were. As a consequence, perhaps, many rushed into marriage, often as a result of whirlwind, wartime romances, and many lived to regret their rashness. The changing attitudes, however, meant that many, trapped in unhappy marriages, no longer felt the need to stay. The divorce rate in Britain has been steadily increasing ever since.

ROMANTIC STORIES

Many women's magazines began to appear at about this time, telling stories of romantic interludes between men and women, often centred in exotic locations; escapism, no doubt, from the humdrum lives of many women, particularly those from poorer backgrounds who were often locked into a life of poverty.

DOOMED ROMANCE

One of the most tragic love affairs in British history occurred at this time. The future Edward VIII met and fell in love with an American, Mrs Wallis Warfield Simpson, on one of his numerous trips to America. She had already divorced one husband and was in the process of divorcing a second when she first met Edward in 1931. However, the Church of England refused to bless the marriage and would not allow a divorcee to be Queen of England. As Edward, once King, would also be head of the English Church, the romance prompted a constitutional crisis. Edward refused to give up Wallis, even after his succession to the throne, so he abdicated, after ruling for just 325 days. Edward and Wallis Simpson left England for France, where they married on 3 June 1937 at the Château de Condé, and remained there in exile until their deaths.

WEDDED BLISS

These two views show the comparative differences between weddings for the middle and working classes in the 1930s. The former (shown right) were very much society affairs, with extensive guest lists, whilst working-class weddings were more low key, with only a handful of guests. They often took place in registry offices because of the cost of hiring a church. Few couples could afford a honeymoon. It was quite common for newly married couples from poorer backgrounds to share the family home of either the bride's or the groom's parents, until they could afford a house of their own.

UNWANTED PREGNANCIES

Surprisingly, as late as the 1930s and 40s, women who gave birth to illegitimate babies (and there were many, especially during the war years) were still looked down upon. Many were shamed into giving their babies up at birth, while many others were brought up by the mother's parents as one of their own children. Some mothers were forced to place their babies in institutions, where they were brought up as orphans. Many of these children, in later life, had to fight for their right to lead independent lives and be released from these institutions.

WAR-TIME ROMANCES

The Second World War saw many couples forge a romance in the heat of the moment. There were many sad farewells or fond homecomings at bus and railway stations, such as this, throughout the war years. Surveys carried out in the early 1940s revealed that 85 percent of married people had experienced a sexual relationship prior to marriage and that half were unfaithful afterwards.

WOMEN & CHILDREN

*T*he Second World War probably had a greater effect on liberating women than any amount of legislation had been able to achieve. They took on many of the jobs formerly done by men (most of whom were called up for service) and even played a major role in the armed forces, not in active service but in auxiliary and support units. The two most striking statistics with regard to women and children at this time were the marked fall in infant and maternal death rates. In 1900 infant mortality was around 142 per 1000 births. By 1938 this figure had fallen to just 55 deaths. Maternal death rates fell from 6 to 3 per 1000 births for the same period.

CHILDREN'S EDUCATION

The 1944 Education Act finally sorted out the anomalies of educating children. After that date all children at both primary and secondary levels could receive free education. It also created a three-tier system of primary schools, secondary schools, and colleges of further education. The leaving age was 15. In 1940 a free school milk scheme was introduced to improve the health of children.

SIMPLE PLEASURES

In the 1930s and 40s the emphasis was on active, rather than passive, leisure time. Children tended to make and find their own amusement. There were no sophisticated electronic or computer games and toys were usually quite simple, made of wood or lead (the latter is now known to be poisonous and has long since been banned in toy production).

WOMEN'S LAND ARMY

Many women signed up to join the 'Women's Land Army'. Often, for city girls, this meant actually leaving home and living on a farm to help with the war effort to keep the nation fed. For this, women received £2.40 per week, of which about half was deducted for their board and lodging. The idea of a women's 'land army' had first been introduced during the First World War, but was reintroduced in earnest during the 1940s.

STREET WISE

In the towns and cities only the fortunate few had gardens in the 1930s. Most working-class houses simply had a backyard with an outside lavatory. Most children had to play in the streets, for there were few playgrounds or recreational areas. Parks were mostly formal and patrolled by park keepers, who were then very authoritarian figures. With little traffic and few crimes against children, the streets were seen as safe playgrounds.

INEQUALITY

Although women had been working in factories for the previous 200 years, they often had to do work that was menial, or beneath male workers. The upsurge of female workers in the 1930s and 40s, particularly in farming and in industry, allowed them to work on equal terms with men, often performing the same tasks. They did not, however, receive the same remuneration. On average, men earned twice as much as women and in some industries, even boys earned more than women doing the same jobs.

SAVIOUR OF THE SKIES

For most Britons, the turning point of the war was the
Battle of Britain in 1940, which many considered was
won by Spitfires, shown here. The Spitfire had a top speed
of 360 mph (579 km/h), and was much more manoeuvrable
than its German counterpart, the Messerschmitt 109.
The RAF was aided by an array of radar stations in south-
east England (the first in the world) which provided the
British pilots with accurate early warning of the approaching enemy aircraft.

HOME GUARD

In the early part of the war, when there was a real threat
of a German invasion, Britain was protected by
several groups of volunteers who acted as air-
raid wardens, fire-watchers and civil defence
volunteers (who later became known as the
Home Guard). They were made up of
citizens who were unable, for a
number of reasons, to join
the armed services.
In addition to defending the home
shores, they were a tremendous
boost to civil moral.

THIS SPECIAL RESPIRATOR
FOR A SMALL CHILD IS
GOVERNMENT PROPERTY.
ANY PERSON WHO HAS IT
IN HIS POSSESSION IS
RESPONSIBLE IN LAW FOR
USING CARE TO KEEP IT IN
GOOD CONDITION. IT IS TO
BE RETURNED TO THE LOCAL
AUTHORITY IN WHOSE
AREA THE POSSESSOR MAY
BE AT ANY TIME, EITHER
ON REQUEST OR WHEN NO
LONGER REQUIRED.

THE 'BLITZ'

Shortly after its defeat in the Battle of Britain,
the German air force resorted to a new technique of
mass-bombing raids, known as the blitzkrieg (or 'blitz') on
British cities. The first raid was on London on 8 September 1940, when 430 citizens died, 1,600
were seriously injured and many thousands made homeless. Many more raids followed, bringing
Britain to its knees. One of the most devastating of all raids was on Coventry, centre of the British
armaments industry, in November 1940 (shown here). In one night, a third of the city was
destroyed and over 4,000 citizens killed.

WAR &
WEAPONRY

The 1930s and 40s were dominated by one single act of war that became, and remains, the most destructive conflict in history, the Second World War. It began in September 1939, when Germany invaded Poland and drew Britain and France, as Poland's allies, into armed conflict with Germany. Hostilities ended in August 1945, but not until some 40 million people had lost their lives. In Britain, a new sense of community spirit developed as everyone 'pulled together' to defeat the common enemy, unprecedented in our history.

RAISING MORALE

George VI took his role as wartime monarch very seriously. He made several morale-boosting visits to the troops abroad during the course of the war, including to Egypt in 1943 (shown here). He even volunteered to accompany the allied invasion forces on D-Day 1944, but Churchill considered it would be too dangerous.

THE WAR OF WARS

More than any other conflict in the history of man, the Second World War directly affected the lives of ordinary people at home, not just the troops in the front line of the conflict. For the first time civilians became a legitimate target, not just to reduce morale of the troops, but to cripple the economy of the country. The Germans launched massed bombing raids against Britain targeting London and the South, as well as other industrialized cities such as Coventry and Liverpool. All families were encouraged to carry gas masks and to build shelters (of corrugated iron protected by mounds of earth) in their gardens, as protection from air raids. Many children in London and the South-east were evacuated to safe refuges in the surrounding country. There they were temporarily 'adopted' by families for the duration of the war.

CRIME & PUNISHMENT

Today, juvenile crime is the fastest growing area of criminal activity. In the 1930s such crime was almost unheard of. In 1938, statistics for the whole of Britain show that just 49 juveniles aged 16 and 737 adolescents aged 17-21 were sent to Borstal institutions. Most crimes (about 95 percent) were theft of property, particularly after the end of the Second World War, when the majority of British fighting troops were demobbed. Some, who were returning to a country where jobs and basic commodities were in short supply, resorted to a life of crime and Britain suffered something of a mini crimewave.

JOHN CHRISTIE

John Christie (1898-1953), of 10 Rillington Place, London, was one of the most notorious mass-murderers of this century. Between 1943 and the early 1950s he murdered several women. He was eventually caught and committed for trial, and was hanged in 1953.

PRISON LIFE

Britain's antiquated prison system could not cope with the sudden influx (47,000 new prisoners a year, on average) after the Second World War. This picture shows new criminals at Strangeways Prison, in Manchester, in 1948.

DEATH PENALTY

At the beginning of the 19th century over 200 different crimes were punishable by death, including petty theft. By the 1930s this had been reduced to just two: premeditated murder and treason. By that time the punishment for all other serious crimes was commuted to long-term prison sentences. Crimes of treason have always been rare, but in 1946 William Joyce (otherwise known as Lord Haw-Haw) was hanged at Wandsworth for broadcasting anti-British propaganda during the Second World War.

THE BLACK MARKET

Perhaps because there was a 'common enemy', or because most of the young men were away fighting, a sense of community spirit prevailed and Britain experienced the lowest recorded crime rates during the Second World War. The most common crime at that time was smuggling and selling goods illegally and without ration coupons on the 'black market'. Many of these goods (including such basic items as food and clothing) were stolen by people working in government supply centres.

ACID BATH MURDERER

John George Haigh (1909-49) was one of the most gruesome criminals of the 1940s, responsible for the death of several people, all murdered for their money. He disposed of his victims' bodies in a vat of acid, earning him the nickname the 'Acid Bath Murderer'. He is seen here leaving the court at Horsham during his trial. He was found guilty and hanged for his crimes in 1949.

POLICEMEN'S BEAT

During the 1930s and 40s the most familiar police activity was constables regularly walking the streets on routine patrols. Their very presence was often sufficient to deter many petty criminals. In the days before computer-based traffic control, the police were often used to direct traffic at busy junctions, as shown here.

TRANSPORT & SCIENCE

CLUES TO THE PAST

In 1947, a method of dating organic material by measuring the amount of radioactive carbon-14 it contained was developed by Willard Libby. Although only accurate within certain parameters, it has become one of the most widely used methods of dating artefacts from the past and buildings associated with them.

*T*here were many advances in science and technology in the 1930s and 40s. Frank Whittle developed the first successful jet engine in 1937. During the war years the engine was developed for fighter aircraft, but it was later adapted for civil use. Also during the war, an arms race developed between Germany and the Allies. German scientists produced the V1 and V2 rockets (known as 'flying bombs') which travelled at speeds in excess of 3,800 mph (6,080 km/h). The advances made in rocketry led directly to the American and Russian space programmes after the war. New materials developed at this time included aluminium, plastic and polythene. The rate of progress in technology continued unabated, even on a more prosaic level; the first ball-point pen was invented in 1938 by Laszlo Biro, a Hungarian, and went on general sale in 1946.

COMMERCIAL AIRLINES

For those who could afford it, a new form of travel, by airliner, became available, significantly reducing travelling time. The first turbo-prop airliner, the Vickers, Viscount, made its maiden flight in 1948.

NUCLEAR TECHNOLOGY

Once it was realized that the nucleus of an atom could be split (as shown), scientists in Britain, America and Europe developed nuclear technology at an alarming rate. Nuclear scientists (many from Germany who fled to America to escape the Nazi regime) developed the first atomic bombs that were dropped on Japan and finally ended the Second World War. Apart from its use as a weapon, nuclear technology developed rapidly after the war, especially in the field of energy.

THE CATSEYE™

The Catseye™ was invented by Percy Shaw in 1934. They significantly reduced road accidents at night by having reflectors mounted into the road surface that are lit up in the headlamp beam of passing motorists.

TRAMWAYS

The most common form of public transport in towns was the tram. Horse-drawn trams (which resembled modern-day buses) were first introduced in the late 19th century, replaced by the 1930s with electric vehicles. They ran on rails embedded in the centre of roads and drew electricity to power the motors from a rotor arm on the roof. These arms connected to overhead cables.

CYCLING

By the 1930s horse-drawn traffic, although it still existed, was disappearing fast. For many, cycles were the principle form of transport, especially for getting to and from work. In pre-war Britain it is estimated there were about 10 million cyclists.

THE AGE OF THE COMPUTER

Early computers were huge machines. They were developed soon after the invention of the transistor in 1947. Much slower than modern computers, they were mostly used for mathematical calculations.

CAR DESIGN

As new types of steel were developed in the 30s and 40s, so it became possible to design cars with curved features, rather than the typical box-like construction of early models. By the end of the 1930s cars had acquired most of the standard features familiar to us today. Developments since then have largely been refinements and improvements in performance.

RELIGION

The 1930s saw a dramatic downturn in the fortunes of the Church and in the number of people who regularly attended services. Having experienced the worst of the Depression many people began to change their values when the upturn in the economy finally came. The 1930s saw the development of mass media and entertainment, when leisure, for the first time in British history, was run as a big business. People began to spend more of their time on leisure pursuits, and on gambling in the hope of never experiencing the hardships of the Depression again. This was at odds with the teaching of the Church and so people began to turn away from organized religion.

THE HYPOCRISY OF WAR

The trend of turning away from the Church continued apace throughout the Second World War. Many who witnessed first-hand the atrocities of man's inhumanity to man turned away from God for allowing such cruelty to happen. Most regiments had their own priest, but many saw their presence on the battlefield as hypocritical.

RASTAFARIAN SECT

In 1930 a new religious sect, the Rastafarians, emerged in Jamaica and has since spread throughout the West Indies and on to Britain. They reject 'white' culture and Christianity, but retain some, if not all, of the Bible. They take their name from Ras Tafari, Emperor of Ethiopia, and regarded by many as the Messiah of the black race. It was one of several alternative religions that have evolved since the 1930s as mainstream religion has gone into decline.

THE DEAD SEA SCROLLS

In 1947 an important religious discovery was made in Israel, which re-affirmed many people's doubts in the authenticity of the Old Testament. A collection of manuscripts, dating from 200 BC, written on scrolls of papyrus and leather were discovered in caves at Qumran, near the Dead Sea (right). They form an almost complete collection of Old Testament writings. Some appear to be written in code and contain some interesting variations to accepted versions of the scriptures.

JEHOVAH'S WITNESSES

In 1931 the 'International Bible Students' Association' changed its name to the more familiar 'Jehovah's Witnesses'. Jehovah is the ancient Hebrew personal name for God. Followers give a percentage of their earnings to the movement. They believe, amongst other things, that they must convert as many people as possible to their beliefs, either by door-to-door canvassing or through their publications, in order to save the human race from self-destruction.

CHANGING TIMES

The Sunday service by 1948 was a scene that was becoming statistically more unusual as congregations continued to dwindle. The Anglican Church suffered most. Chapel-oers in Wales, Presbyterians n Scotland, and Catholics hroughout the country managed to keep higher ttendance levels, as they ill do.

DID YOU KNOW?

That the Germans invented a new word to describe cities destroyed by bombing? Following the Battle of Britain, Germany began massed bombing raids on strategic British cities. London was the first target, but Coventry sustained a prolonged air raid lasting some 10 hours. One third of the city was destroyed and over 4,000 people were killed. Delighted with the success of their mission, the Germans coined a new verb to describe such destruction: Coventrieren – 'to coventrize'.

That British inventiveness made the D-Day landings possible? In June 1944 the Allies coordinated a massive landing of troops and equipment on Normandy beaches. The Germans had built a wall of defences along the Atlantic coastline and made all French ports impregnable. However, the British had invented a floating harbour, called a 'Mulberry'. They towed two of these artificial harbours across the Channel and so began 'Operation Overlord'.

That an RAF gunner fell 18,000 feet from his aeroplane and lived? During an air raid by the RAF over Germany, gunner Sergeant Nicholas Alkemade's Lancaster bomber was hit by enemy fire. The plane caught fire and, with no time to put on a parachute, he made the split-second decision to jump out of the bomber rather than burn to death. He jumped out at 18,000 feet (5,484 metres) but landed uninjured and still conscious a few moments later. He fell at a rate of 120 mph but his fall was broken by the springy branches of pine trees and deep snow.

That Kilroy really was 'ere? Ever since the Second World War the phrase 'Kilroy was 'ere' has been emblazoned on walls by graffiti artists. James J. Kilroy was an American shipyard inspector who signed his name in chalk as proof that something was satisfactory. So thorough was he that his signature appeared in the most unlikely places on the ships he inspected. It thus became a humorous quip with soldiers that no matter in what remote spot in the world they found themselves, Kilroy was bound to have been there first. The craze for scribbling his name on walls caught on throughout the English-speaking world.

That the Germans' own obsession for detail helped the Allies to win the war? Just prior to the outbreak of the war the Polish Secret Service handed to Britain a machine stolen from the Third Reich. It was called Enigma and resembled a small typewriter. In fact, it was a complex encoding machine which the Germans used to transmit all their top secret messages. The difficult task of British Intelligence officers to decipher the messages was made easier by the Germans' insistence on being methodical and logical. British decoders were therefore able to eliminate many of the possible codes. Details of Britain's possession of the Enigma machine were not released until the 1970s and even Allied commanders during the war were unaware of its existence.

ACKNOWLEDGEMENTS

We would like to thank: Graham Rich, Hazel Poole and Elizabeth Wiggans for their assistance.
Copyright © 2006 ticktock Entertainment Ltd.
First published in Great Britain by *ticktock* Media Ltd., Unit 2, Orchard Business Centre, North Farm Road, Tunbridge Wells, Kent, TN2 3EH, U.K.
All rights reserved. No part of this publication may be reproduced, stored in a retrieval system, or transmitted in any form or by any means electronic, mechanical, photocopying, recording or otherwise, without prior written permission of the copyright owner.
A CIP catalogue record for this book is available from the British Library. ISBN 1 86007 407 3
Picture research by Image Select. Printed in Hong Kong.

INDEX

30s & 40s BRITAIN

A comprehensive, informative and highly readable introduction to life in 30s and 40s Britain.

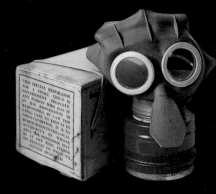

Written by John Guy, an expert in the field, this book is based on the very latest research.

Over 100 beautiful colour images and illustrations bring the 30s and 40s back to life, keeping you hooked until you reach the end of the book.

£3.99

ISBN 1-86007-407-3

9 781860 074073